Westminster
Shorter Catechism
for Kids

Westminster
Shorter Catechism
for Kids

_____

Workbook One: Who is God?
Questions 1 – 10

_____

Caroline Weerstra

Catechism for Kids
Visit our website
www.commonlifepress.org

The solutions manual for this workbook is available
for FREE download from Common Life Press.

www.commonlifepress.org

For more information on this workbook series, email:
info@commonlifepress.org

Contents

Introduction

When I began homeschooling my daughter Kaylee, I decided that it was time to begin her training in the Westminster Shorter Catechism. I set aside her little Bible storybooks with the cartoonish illustrations. I plunked a full-sized Bible in front of her, printed out a copy of the Westminster Shorter Catechism, and told her it was time to begin studying the big-girl lessons.

She was excited until she began to read the Shorter Catechism. "Mom," she said, wrinkling her forehead in confusion. "I don't understand any of this. What is a 'chief end'? What does 'infinite' mean? And I can't even pronounce this word ..." She pointed at 'fore-ordained.'

"Ah, yes, well ..." I thought for a moment. "Don't worry, Kaylee. I'm sure that there are workbooks that explain everything. I will buy you some."

She smiled confidently. "Good!" she said. "It's weird trying to memorize something when I don't even know what it means."

I spent the next three hours scanning every online bookstore and homeschool curriculum website I could find. I called friends. I emailed homeschool support groups. In the end, I had to admit defeat. A curriculum such as I had in mind apparently did not even exist!

I reluctantly returned to my daughter with the dismal news.

"Well, Mom," she said, "do *you* understand the Westminster Shorter Catechism?"

"Yes, I believe I do."

"Well, why don't you write my worksheets?"

And so began our catechism project. Kaylee drank in Westminster Shorter Catechism with great enthusiasm. She loved learning the new words. I found great joy in teaching her to evaluate theological concepts and to appreciate the wisdom handed down to us over the centuries by the church fathers. Church history, great theological works, and original text languages could be introduced to her thinking—not in completeness, of course, but enough to pique her interest for future studies of the foundations of her faith.

As our project progressed, I began to receive emails and calls from other mothers who were interested in our program. "Can you tell me where you got those catechism worksheets that your daughter is using?"

And so this workbook series has come to fruition. I hope and pray that it is a blessing to many other dear covenant children who are eager to study the tenets of their faith but may be hampered by big words and difficult concepts. May they feast their minds on the richness of God's Word and the teaching of the Westminster Shorter Catechism, and may it lead to a lifetime of understanding.

This workbook is designed to familiarize the child with the Westminster Shorter Catechism and assist in memorization. Repetition is key. Each catechism section is repeated several times over the course of several lessons.

Workbook lessons contain fill-in-the-blank questions which require students to display their comprehension of the lesson. Additionally, there are *Let's Think* portions which encourage a deeper contemplation of the material and application to life situations. Instructors should take time to discuss and think through these questions with the child. The goal is that a child would remember the catechism, understand it, and have the ability to apply the biblical principles to Christian life.

The Westminster Shorter Catechism begins with momentous questions about the purpose of life and the nature of God. From there, it moves into a discussion of sin and misery, and then it shows us our Savior. Finally, it presents the Ten Commandments, the sacraments, and the Lord's Prayer. The catechism is a summary of Christian life and doctrine from one end to the other, packed tightly into 107 questions and answers. Every word of the Shorter Catechism is carefully and lovingly crafted to turn the heart of the reader toward Christ and his Word.

We are greatly blessed to have the Westminster Shorter Catechism as a tool for teaching our children. These workbooks will never do justice to the beautiful language and elegant contemplation found within the

Westminster Shorter Catechism. However, if these pages assist children toward a better appreciation for and understanding of it, then I am grateful.

Caroline Weerstra
Catechism for Kids
Schenectady, New York

Question 1: What is the chief end of man?

Answer: Man's chief end is to glorify God, and to enjoy him forever.

Lesson 1

Question 1: What is the chief end of man?

Answer: Man's chief end is to glorify God, and to enjoy him forever.

 **Q. 1. What is the chief end of man?**

A.

_____

_____

Our Main Purpose

What does 'chief end' mean? 'Chief end' means 'main purpose.' The main purpose of man is to glorify God and to enjoy him forever.

Why does the catechism say 'man'? What about women? The word 'man' in the Shorter Catechism is talking about all humans— men, women, and children. The main purpose of all people is to glorify God and to enjoy him forever.

 **Fill in the blanks.**

What is your main purpose?

My main purpose is to _____ _____

and to _____ him forever.

How long will you enjoy God?

I will enjoy God _____.

Lesson 2

Q. 1. What is the chief end of man?

A. Man's chief end is to _____ God, and to

_____ him forever.

To Glorify God

The Westminster Shorter Catechism summarizes the Bible in a way that is easy to understand and remember. The Bible tells us that our main purpose is to glorify God:

I Corinthians 10:31 So whether you eat or drink or whatever you do, do it all for the glory of God.

This verse tells us that whatever we do, we should always do it to honor and glorify God. Whether you are at home, school, or church, you should always obey God's commandments. We should remember God in everything we do.

The Bible also tells us that our other main purpose is to enjoy God forever. Let's read:

Psalm 73:25-26 Whom have I in heaven but you? And earth has nothing I desire besides you. My flesh and my heart may fail, but God is the strength of my heart and my portion forever.

In this psalm, the songwriter says that he knows God is with him always, even when he feels weak and afraid. We can see that the psalmist loves and enjoys God. He says that the whole earth has nothing he wants besides God.

 Let's Think!

Can you think of any other Bible verse which speaks about glorifying or enjoying God? Which one do you remember?

_____

How do you glorify God at home?

_____

_____

How to do you glorify God at church?

_____

_____

How do you glorify God while doing your chores?

_____

_____

How do you glorify God while playing with your friends?

_____

_____

Draw a picture of something you do that glorifies God:

Lesson 3

Q. 1. What is the chief end of man?

A. Man's _____ _____ is to

_____ God, and to _____

him _____.

A Parable

The main purpose of all men, women, and children is to glorify and enjoy God. However, some people think that the main purpose of life is to have a lot of money or other nice things. Why are they wrong?

Jesus told a story about people who think that the main purpose of life is to obtain money and nice things. Let's read the story:

Luke 12:16-21 The ground of a certain rich man produced a good crop. He thought to himself, "What shall I do? I have no place to store my crops." Then he said, "This is what I'll do. I will tear down my barns and build bigger ones, and there I will store all my grain and my goods. And I'll say to myself, 'You have plenty of good things laid up for many years. Take life easy; eat, drink and be merry.'" But God said to him, "You fool! This very night your life will be demanded from you. Then who will get what you have prepared for yourself?" This is how it will be with anyone who stores up things for himself but is not rich toward God.

Let's Think!

Was it wrong for the rich man to build a bigger barn? _____

Who made the rich man? _____

Who gave the rich man his crops? _____

Who decided when the rich man would die? _____

Was the rich man thinking about God? _____

Why did God call the rich man a fool? _____

_____

Question 2: What rule hath God given to direct us how we may glorify and enjoy him?

Answer: The Word of God, which is contained in the Scriptures of the Old and New Testaments, is the only rule to direct us how we may glorify and enjoy him.

Lesson 1

> Question 2: What rule hath God given to direct us how we may glorify and enjoy him?
>
> Answer: The Word of God, which is contained in the Scriptures of the Old and New Testaments, is the only rule to direct us how we may glorify and enjoy him.

Q. 2. What rule hath God given to direct us how we may glorify and enjoy him?

A.

_____

_____

_____

The Bible

What is the Word of God (Scripture)? The Bible is the Word of God (Scripture).

Who wrote the Bible? The Bible was written by holy men who were instructed by the Holy Spirit. They wrote as the Holy Spirit taught them.

Why does the catechism say 'hath'? 'Hath' is an old-fashioned way of saying 'has.' The question could be said like this: *What rule has God given to teach us how to glorify and enjoy him?*

 **Fill in the blanks.**

Can we do whatever we want and say that we are glorifying God?

_____

What did God give us to teach us how to glorify and enjoy him?

_____

We call the Bible the 'Word of God.' What else do we call it?

_____

Lesson 2

Q. 2. What rule hath God given to direct us how we may glorify and enjoy him?

A. The _____ of God, which is contained in the

Scriptures of the _____ and _____ Testaments,

is the only _____ to direct us how we may glorify and

_____ him.

Who Wrote the Bible?

The Bible says Scripture is our guide to glorifying and enjoying God. Let's read:

Ephesians 2:20 built on the foundation of the apostles and prophets, with Christ Jesus himself as the chief cornerstone.

The apostles and the prophets were the holy men who were instructed by the Holy Spirit. They wrote the Scriptures as God commanded them.

We read the Bible to learn how to glorify and enjoy God. Ephesians 2:20 compares the church to a house. The foundation of our 'house' is made up of the words of the apostles and the prophets (which we can read in the Bible). Later, God added us to his church. We are built on the firm foundation of Scripture.

A cornerstone is the very first and most important piece of a house. Every other part of the house is built in reference to the cornerstone. In our 'house,' the cornerstone is Christ Jesus.

The apostle Paul wrote to his friend Timothy about how important Scripture is to us:

II Timothy 3:16 All Scripture is God-breathed and is useful for teaching, rebuking, correcting and training in righteousness.

All Scripture (both the Old Testament and the New Testament) is from God. In fact, it is so directly from God that it is like God breathed it out on us. The Word of God is useful for teaching people, training them to do right, and correcting them when they go the wrong way or when they do not obey God as they should.

Like Paul, John was an apostle. Paul and John were two of the holy men who wrote the Bible as the Holy Spirit taught them. John saw the miracles that Jesus performed and heard the words that Jesus spoke.

I John 1:3 We proclaim to you what we have seen and heard, so that you also may have fellowship with us. And our fellowship is with the Father and with his Son, Jesus Christ.

Let's Think!

Who wrote the Bible? _____

_____

Who were some of the holy men who wrote as the Holy Spirit taught them?

_____

_____

How did John know that the things he said about Jesus were true?

_____

_____

What makes the Bible more special than other books?

_____

Lesson 3

Q. 2. What rule hath God given to direct us how we may glorify and enjoy him?

A. The _____ of God, which is contained in the

Scriptures of the _____ and _____ _____,

is the only _____ to direct us how we may _____

and _____ him.

Books of the Bible

Do you know the books of the Bible? Let's study them! In the next few pages, you will read a poem that was written in the early 20th century. No one knows who wrote it, but it may help you remember the books of the Bible.

The Old Testament is made up of several major parts: the books of Moses (also called the Pentateuch), the historical books, the devotional books, and the prophets. The New Testament is composed of the gospels, the book of Acts, and the epistles (letters).

Books of the Bible

Old Testament

In Genesis, the world was made,
In Exodus, the march is told;
Leviticus contains the law;
In Numbers are the tribes enrolled.

In Deuteronomy again,
We're urged to keep God's law alone;
And these five books of Moses make
The oldest holy writing known.

* * * * *

Brave Joshua to Canaan leads;
In Judges, oft the Jews rebel;
We read of David's name in Ruth
And First and Second Samuel.

In First and Second Kings, we read
How bad the Hebrew state became;
In First and Second Chronicles
Another history of the same.

In Ezra, captive Jews return,
And Nehemiah builds the wall;
Queen Esther saves her race from death.
The books 'historical' we call.

* * * * *

In Job, we read of patient faith;
In Psalms are David's songs of praise;
The proverbs are to make us wise;
Ecclesiastes next portrays

How fleeting earthly pleasures are;
The Song of Solomon is all
About true love, like Christ's; and these
Five books "devotional" we call.

*   *   *   *   *

Isaiah tells of Christ to come,
While Jeremiah tells of woe,
And in his Lamentations mourns
The Holy City's overthrow.

Ezekiel speaks of mysteries,
And Daniel foretells kings of old;
Hosea over Israel grieves;
In Joel, blessings are foretold.

In Amos, too, are Israel's woes,
And Obadiah's sent to warn,
While Jonah shows that Christ should die,
And Micah where he should be born.

In Nahum, Ninevah is seen;
Habakkuk tells of Chaldea's guilt;
In Zephaniah are Judah's sins;
In Haggai, the Temple's built.

Then Zechariah speaks of Christ,
And Malachi, his sign;
The prophets number seventeen,
And all the books are thirty-nine.

New Testament

Matthew, Mark, Luke, and John
Tell what Christ did in every place.
The Acts tell what the apostles did,
And Romans how we're saved by grace.

Corinthians instructs the church;
Galatians shows us faith alone,
Ephesians, true love, and in
Philippians, God's grace is shown

Colossians tells us more of Christ,
And Thessalonians of the end;
In Timothy and Titus both
Are rules for pastors to attend.

Philemon Christian friendship shows,
Then Hebrews clearly tells how all
The Jewish law prefigured Christ.
Most of these epistles are by Paul.

James shows that faith by works must live,
And Peter urges steadfastness,
While John exhorts to Christian love,
For those who have it God will bless.

Jude shows the end of evil men,
And Revelation tells of heaven.
This ends the whole New Testament,
And all the books are twenty-seven.

 **Fill in the blank.**

How many books are in the Old Testament? _____

How many books are in the New Testament? _____

What are the four main parts of the Old Testament?

1. _____

2. _____

3. _____

4. _____

Most epistles in the New Testament were written by _____.

Question 3: What do the Scriptures principally teach?

Answer: The Scriptures principally teach what man is to believe concerning God, and what duty God requires of man.

Lesson 1

Question 3: What do the Scriptures principally teach?

Answer: The Scriptures principally teach what man is to believe concerning God, and what duty God requires of man.

Q. 3. What do the Scriptures principally teach?

A.

_____

_____

Our Duty

What does 'principally' mean? 'Principally' means 'mostly.' The Bible teaches a lot of things, but mostly, it focuses on what people should believe about God and how we should obey God.

What is a duty? A **duty** is something we must do in order to do the right thing. For example, it is the duty of a father to provide for his children. It is the duty of children to obey their parents. And it is the duty of all people to honor God.

 **Fill in the blanks.**

The Scriptures mostly teach what we should _____

about God and what _____ God requires of us.

The Scriptures include both the _____ Testament and

the _____ Testament.

Draw a picture of something that is your duty:

Lesson 2

Q. 3. What do the Scriptures principally teach?

A. The _____ principally _____ what

man is to _____ concerning God, and what duty

God requires of _____.

 Let's Think!

Do you remember the Ten Commandments? (If you do not remember them, you can read them in Exodus 20:1-17).

List the Ten Commandments:

1.

_____

2.

_____

3.

_____

4.

_____

5.

_____

6.

_____

7.

_____

8.

_____

9.

_____

10.

_____

The Ten Commandments are all duties which God requires of us. These are very important rules, and we will discuss them much more in Workbook Five and Workbook Six of this series.

Question 4: What is God?

Answer: God is a Spirit, infinite, eternal, and unchangeable, in his being, wisdom, power, holiness, justice, goodness, and truth.

Lesson 1

Question 4: What is God?

Answer: God is a Spirit, infinite, eternal, and unchangeable, in his being, wisdom, power, holiness, justice, goodness, and truth.

 **Q. 4. What is God?**

A.

_____

_____

_____

Attributes of God

This is a very important section of the catechism because it teaches the **attributes of God** (what God is like). God is strong, good, and wise. He always does the right thing, and he always speaks the truth.

Although it is very important, this part of the catechism can be a little difficult to understand. Let's take it one piece at a time:

What does 'infinite' mean? 'Infinite' means something is so big that there is no end to it.

What does 'eternal' mean? 'Eternal' means something always existed and will always exist.

What does 'unchangeable' mean? 'Unchangeable' means something cannot be changed.

The Shorter Catechism applies each of these characteristics to the attributes of God (see chart on page 38). Everything in God's nature is infinite, eternal, and unchangeable. God's **being** is infinite, eternal, and unchangeable. His **wisdom** is infinite, eternal, and unchangeable. His **power** is infinite, eternal, and unchangeable. We could go on to say the same about each of God's attributes.

 Let's Think!

If you are afraid, what can you remember about God's attributes?

_____

When people do bad things, they often imagine that God will not do anything to punish them. What should they remember about God's attributes?

_____

	INFINITE	ETERNAL	UNCHANGEABLE
BEING	**INFINITE BEING** God is so big that nothing can contain him. There is no place without God.	**ETERNAL BEING** God has always existed and will always exist.	**UNCHANGEABLE BEING** God does not change. He will never grow smaller or become something else.
WISDOM	**INFINITE WISDOM** God knows everything. He always makes good decisions.	**ETERNAL WISDOM** God has always been wise and will always be wise.	**UNCHANGEABLE WISDOM** God's wisdom does not change. He does not forget things or become foolish.
POWER	**INFINITE POWER** God is so strong that he can do anything. No one can stand against God.	**ETERNAL POWER** God has always been strong and mighty, and he will always be strong and mighty.	**UNCHANGEABLE POWER** God's power does not change.
HOLINESS	**INFINITE HOLINESS** God never sins. He always does the right thing.	**ETERNAL HOLINESS** God has never sinned, and he will never sin.	**UNCHANGEABLE HOLINESS** God's holiness does not change. He will never become sinful.
JUSTICE	**INFINITE JUSTICE** God is always fair in his decisions.	**ETERNAL JUSTICE** God has always been fair, and he will always be fair. In the end, he will make everything right.	**UNCHANGEABLE JUSTICE** God will never change to become unfair.
GOODNESS	**INFINITE GOODNESS** God's goodness is endless. He is always good in everything he does.	**ETERNAL GOODNESS** God has always been good, and he will always be good.	**UNCHANGEABLE GOODNESS** God will never change in his goodness. He will never become evil. He will always be good.
TRUTH	**INFINITE TRUTH** God never lies. He always speaks the truth. We can always believe what he says.	**ETERNAL TRUTH** God has always been truthful, and he will always be truthful.	**UNCHANGEABLE TRUTH** God will never change, and his Word never changes. We can always trust God.

Lesson 2

Q. 4. What is God?

A. God is a _____, infinite, _____, and

unchangeable, in his _____, wisdom, _____,

holiness, _____, goodness, and _____.

What is God?

Remember that the Westminster Shorter Catechism summarizes the teaching of Scripture. Let's look at some Bible verses which discuss the attributes of God.

 **After each verse, fill in the attribute to which it is referring.**

John 4:24 God is spirit, and his worshipers must worship in spirit and in truth.

God is a _____, infinite, eternal and unchangeable in his being, wisdom, power, holiness, justice, goodness, and truth.

Job 11:7 Can you fathom the mysteries of God? Can you probe the limits of the Almighty?

God is a Spirit, _____, eternal and unchangeable in his being, wisdom, power, holiness, justice, goodness, and truth.

Psalm 90:2 Before the mountains were born or you brought forth the earth and the world, from everlasting to everlasting you are God.

God is a Spirit, infinite, _____ and unchangeable in his being, wisdom, power, holiness, justice, goodness, and truth.

James 1:17 Every good and perfect gift is from above, coming down from the Father of the heavenly lights, who does not change like shifting shadows.

God is a Spirit, infinite, eternal and _____ in his being, wisdom, power, holiness, justice, goodness, and truth.

Exodus 3:14 God said to Moses, "I am who I am. This is what you are to say to the Israelites: 'I AM has sent me to you.'"

God is a Spirit, infinite, eternal and unchangeable in his

_____, wisdom, power, holiness, justice, goodness, and truth.

> **Psalm 147:5** Great is our Lord and mighty in power; his understanding has no limit.

God is a Spirit, infinite, eternal and unchangeable in his being,

_____, _____, holiness, justice, goodness, and truth.

> **Isaiah 6:1-3** In the year that King Uzziah died, I saw the Lord seated on a throne, high and exalted, and the train of his robe filled the temple. Above him were seraphs, each with six wings: with two wings they covered their faces, with two they covered their feet, and with two they were flying. And they were calling to one another: "Holy, holy, holy is the LORD Almighty; the whole earth is full of his glory."

God is a Spirit, infinite, eternal and unchangeable in his being,

wisdom, power, _____, justice, goodness, and truth.

> **Exodus 34:5-7** Then the LORD came down in the cloud and stood there with him and proclaimed his name, the LORD. And he passed in front of Moses, proclaiming, "The LORD, the LORD, the

compassionate and gracious God, slow to anger, abounding in love and faithfulness, maintaining love to thousands, and forgiving wickedness, rebellion, and sin. Yet he does not leave the guilty unpunished; he punishes the children and their children for the sins of the fathers to the third and fourth generation."

God is a Spirit, infinite, eternal and unchangeable in his being,

wisdom, power, holiness, _____, _____, and truth.

Numbers 23:19 God is not a man, that he should lie, nor a son of man, that he should change his mind. Does he speak and then not act? Does he promise and not fulfill?

God is a Spirit, infinite, eternal and unchangeable in his being,

wisdom, power, holiness, justice, goodness, and _____.

Question 5: Are there more Gods than one?

Answer: There is but one only, the living and true God.

Lesson 1

> Question 5: Are there more Gods than one?
>
> Answer: There is but one only, the living and true God.

 **Q. 5. Are there more Gods than one?**

A.

_____

_____

One God

This is an easy catechism section with no big words! It is simple: there is only one God, the living and true God. Any other gods that people may worship do not exist.

Many people even today worship idols (statues or paintings) which they believe represent their gods. Let's read what the Bible says about those gods:

> **Psalm 135:15-18** The idols of the nations are silver and gold, made by human hands. They have mouths, but cannot speak, eyes, but

cannot see. They have ears, but cannot hear, nor is there breath in their mouths. Those who make them will be like them, and so will all who trust in them.

 # Let's Think!

According to the psalm, who makes idols? _____

Do the eyes, ears, and mouth of an idol have any use? _____

Is the idol able to do anything? _____

How are idols different from the real God? _____

_____

Some Christians are afraid to see a picture of an idol because they worry that it might hurt them. Will looking at an idol hurt them?

_____

Why should we never be afraid of an idol? _____

_____

Should we ever worship an idol? Why or why not?

_____

_____

Lesson 2

Q. 5. Are there more Gods than one?

A. There is but _____ only, the living and true _____.

Elijah and the Prophets of Baal

The book of Kings tells a wonderful story about a time when the people of Israel were not sure whether God was the one true God. Some other people living around them worshiped an idol called Baal. The Israelites started worshiping Baal as well. Elijah, the prophet of God, called the people of Israel to meet with him.

I Kings 18:21-39 Elijah went before the people and said, "How long will you waver between two opinions? If the LORD is God, follow him; but if Baal is God, follow him."

But the people said nothing.

Then Elijah said to them, "I am the only one of the LORD's prophets left, but Baal has four hundred and fifty prophets. Get two bulls for us. Let Baal's prophets choose one for themselves, and let them cut it into pieces and put it on the wood but not set fire to it. I will prepare the other bull and put it on the wood but not set fire to it. Then you call on the name of your god, and I will call on the name of the LORD. The god who answers by fire—he is God."

Then all the people said, "What you say is good."

Elijah said to the prophets of Baal, "Choose one of the bulls and prepare it first, since there are so many of you. Call on the name of your god, but do not light the fire." So they took the bull given them and prepared it.

Then they called on the name of Baal from morning till noon. "Baal, answer us!" they shouted. But there was no response; no one answered. And they danced around the altar they had made.

At noon Elijah began to taunt them. "Shout louder!" he said. "Surely he is a god! Perhaps he is deep in thought, or busy, or traveling. Maybe he is sleeping and must be awakened." So they shouted louder and slashed themselves with swords and spears, as was their custom, until their blood flowed. Midday passed, and they continued their frantic prophesying until the time for the evening sacrifice. But there was no response, no one answered, no one paid attention.

Then Elijah said to all the people, "Come here to me." They came to him, and he repaired the altar of the LORD, which had been torn down. Elijah took twelve stones, one for each of the tribes descended from Jacob, to whom the word of the LORD had come, saying, "Your name shall be Israel." With the stones he built an altar in the name of the LORD, and he dug a trench around it large enough to hold two seahs of seed. He arranged the wood, cut the bull into pieces and laid it on the wood. Then he said to them, "Fill four large jars with water and pour it on the offering and on the wood."

"Do it again," he said, and they did it again.

"Do it a third time," he ordered, and they did it the third time. The water ran down around the altar and even filled the trench.

At the time of sacrifice, the prophet Elijah stepped forward and prayed: "LORD, the God of Abraham, Isaac and Israel, let it be known today that you are God in Israel and that I am your servant and have done all these things at your command. Answer me, LORD, answer me, so these people will know that you, LORD, are

God, and that you are turning their hearts back again."

Then the fire of the LORD fell and burned up the sacrifice, the wood, the stones and the soil, and also licked up the water in the trench.

When all the people saw this, they fell prostrate and cried, "The LORD—he is God! The LORD—he is God!"

 # Let's Think!

Do you think the prophets of Baal really thought Baal was a god? Why or why not?

_____

_____

Why did Elijah pour water on the altar?

_____

Did Elijah have to do anything crazy like shout or cut himself so that God would hear him?

_____

_____

Why did Elijah have victory over the prophets of Baal?

_____

_____

Lesson 3

> Q. 5. Are there more Gods than one?
>
> A. There is but _____ only, the _____ and
>
> true _____.

The Sh'ma

A famous verse in the book of Deuteronomy proclaims that there is only one God:

> **Deuteronomy 6:4**   Hear, O Israel: The LORD our God, the LORD is one.

In Hebrew (the original language of the Old Testament), this verse is called the **Sh'ma**. It is referred to that way because the word **sh'ma** in Hebrew means 'hear,' and that is how the verse begins. The Hebrew language reads right-to-left (instead of left-to-right as English does).   Here is the Sh'ma in Hebrew:

שְׁמַע יִשְׂרָאֵל יְהוָה אֱלֹהֵינוּ יְהוָה אֶחָד

The Sh'ma is pronounced like this:

Sh'ma Yishrael: Adonai Eloheinu Adonai Echad

Throughout generations, God reminded his people again and again that there is only one God. The Israelites kept wandering away to worship other gods, which are not really gods at all. The prophet Jeremiah warned God's people:

Jeremiah 10:14-16 Everyone is senseless and without knowledge; every goldsmith is shamed by his idols. The images he makes are a fraud; they have no breath in them. They are worthless, the objects of mockery; when their judgment comes, they will perish. He who is the Portion of Jacob is not like these, for he is the Maker of all things, including Israel, the people of his inheritance— the LORD Almighty is his name.

 Let's Think!

What warning did Jeremiah give to God's people about the images they were making?

_____

_____

How is the true God different from an image made by a goldsmith?

_____

Look up the Sh'ma (Deuteronomy 6:4) in your Bible. What is the next verse (Deuteronomy 6:5)?

_____

_____

Deuteronomy 6:5 is quoted in the New Testament. Who quoted it?

_____

Question 6: How many persons are there in the Godhead?

Answer: There are three persons in the Godhead: the Father, the Son, and the Holy Spirit; and these three are one God, the same in substance, equal in power and glory.

Lesson 1

Question 6: How many persons are there in the Godhead?

Answer: There are three persons in the Godhead: the Father, the Son, and the Holy Spirit; and these three are one God, the same in substance, equal in power and glory.

Q. 6. How many persons are there in the Godhead?

A.

_____

_____

_____

_____

_____

The Trinity

God is one God, but he is also three Persons—the Father, the Son, and the Holy Spirit. Each of the Persons of the Godhead is completely God. Each is equal with the others in power and glory. None of the Persons of the Trinity is bigger, smaller, more powerful, less powerful, or composed of something different than the other Persons of the Godhead.

Fill in the blanks.

Is the Father God? _____

Is the Son God? _____

Is the Holy Spirit God? _____

How many Gods are there? _____

How many Persons are in the Godhead? _____

Who is the Son? _____

Lesson 2

Q. 6. How many persons are there in the Godhead?

A. There are _____ persons in the _____:

the Father, the _____, and the _____ _____;

and these three are one _____, the same in substance,

equal in _____ and glory.

Arius and Athanaseus

The three-in-one concept that we discussed in the last lesson is called the **Trinity**. It is not easy to understand. In fact, we often describe it as a **mystery**. We realize that we do not comprehend everything about God, but we believe what he tells us about himself. If we cannot quite imagine how God can be one God and three Persons, then we must recognize that our minds are small compared to God. He knows everything. He understands everything. We do not know or understand everything, but we trust that God speaks the truth.

In the early days of the church, many people were confused about the Trinity. Some people thought Jesus was not completely God or that he had not always existed. Finally, the church held a council at Nicaea in 325 AD to discuss the matter and better understand it. The two predominant views were represented by Arius and Athanaseus (among others).

Arius argued that Jesus had not always existed but that the Father had created Jesus out of nothing. Arius claimed that Jesus could not be of the same substance as the Father.

Athanaseus explained that Jesus is the same substance as the Father. He declared that Jesus is eternal and equal in power and glory with the Father. Why did Athanaseus believe this? Because Jesus said so (John 8:58), and if Jesus was not who he said he was, then he could not have saved us from our sins. Athanaseus believed God's Word. He knew that he could always trust God.

The council discussed each of the views and concluded that Athanaseus was correct. They wrote a creed explaining the doctrine of the Trinity:

Nicene Creed (325 AD)

We believe in one God the Father Almighty,
Maker of all things visible and invisible;
and in one Lord Jesus Christ,
the only begotten of the Father,
that is, of the substance of the Father,
God of God,
light of light,
true God of true God,
begotten, not made,
of the same substance with the Father,
through whom all things were made both in heaven and on earth;
who for us men and our salvation descended,

was incarnate, and was made man,
suffered and rose again the third day,
ascended into heaven,
and cometh to judge the living and the dead.
And we believe in the Holy Spirit.
Those who say:
There was a time when he was not,
and he was not before he was made;
and that he was made out of nothing;
or who maintain that he is of another substance
or essence than the Father,
or that the Son of God is created,
or changeable, or alterable —
These the church condemns.

There is a more famous Nicene Creed which was written later, but this earlier version was composed and signed by the council in 325 AD. Notice that it condemns Arius and his followers, and it clearly proclaims that Jesus is the same substance as the Father.

 **Fill in the blanks.**

The doctrine which teaches that God is one God and also

three Persons is called the _____. At the Council of

_____ in 325 AD, the proper view of the Trinity was

presented by _____. The council agreed

with Athanaseus and wrote a _____ declaring

that Jesus is the same in substance as the _____.

Lesson 3

Q. 6. How many persons are there in the Godhead?

A. There are three _____ in the _____:

the _____, the _____, and the Holy Spirit; and

these three are _____ God, the _____ in

substance, equal in _____ and _____.

Father, Son, and Holy Spirit

Jesus spoke of the Trinity to his disciples after his resurrection before he ascended into heaven. He gave them this command:

Matthew 28:19 Therefore go and make disciples of all nations, baptizing them in the name of the Father and of the Son and of the Holy Spirit.

Baptism marks us as God's people. In this Bible verse, we are told how we are to be baptized—in the name of the Father, the Son, and the Holy Spirit.

 ## Let's Think!

What words does a minister speak when he baptizes someone?

_____

_____

What does this baptismal formula mean?

_____

_____

Question 7: What are the decrees of God?

Answer: The decrees of God are his eternal purpose, according to the counsel of his will, whereby, for his own glory, he hath fore-ordained whatsoever comes to pass.

Lesson 1

Question 7: What are the decrees of God?

Answer: The decrees of God are his eternal purpose, according to the counsel of his will, whereby, for his own glory, he hath fore-ordained whatsoever comes to pass.

Q. 7. What are the decrees of God?

A.

_____

_____

_____

_____

The Decrees of God

This is another very important section of the catechism with a lot of big words!

Do you remember what 'eternal' means? If not, look back at page 37.

Eternal means _____.

Let's consider the first piece of the catechism answer.

> ### The decrees of God are his eternal purpose.

This part tells us that the decrees of God are purposes which last forever and ever. God always determines what will happen, and his decrees do not change.

What does 'counsel' mean? The word 'counsel' (in this context) means 'plan.'

What does 'will' mean? In this context, 'will' means 'desire' or 'choice.'

Let's put together what we have defined so far:

> ### The decrees of God are his eternal purpose, according to the counsel of his will.

The decrees of God are purposes that last forever and ever, and he plans these things according to what he wants to happen. God does not go around asking people for advice. He does not ask anyone whether they think his plan is a good idea. He makes all the decisions himself. Remember that God is **infinitely wise**, and so all his decisions are good decisions.

What does 'whereby' mean? 'Whereby' is an old word which means that this is how something happens.

What does 'fore-ordained' mean? 'Fore' is a prefix which means 'before,' and 'ordained' means something has been chosen by God. 'Fore-ordained' indicates that God has chosen something before it occurs.

What does 'whatsoever' mean? 'Whatsoever' means 'everything.'

What do we mean when we say that something 'comes to pass'? When we say that something 'comes to pass,' we mean that it happens.

Now we know what all the words mean, so let's put the whole sentence together:

> **The decrees of God are his eternal purpose, according to the counsel of his will, whereby, for his own glory, he hath fore-ordained whatsoever comes to pass.**

The decrees of God are purposes that last forever and ever, and he plans these things according to what he wants to happen. This is how (for his own glory) he has chosen everything that happens before it occurs.

We often refer to this concept as the **sovereignty of God**. God is King over the universe and beyond. He rules over everything. He plans everything before it happens. In fact, everything happens because God has already **decreed** that it will happen.

 **Fill in the blanks.**

For how long do God's purposes last? _____

Who does God ask for advice? _____

How many things does God plan? _____

What do we mean when we talk about the sovereignty of God?

_____

_____

Lesson 2

Q. 7. What are the decrees of God?

A. The _____ of God are his _____

purpose, according to the _____ of his _____,

whereby, for his own _____, he hath fore-ordained

whatsoever comes to _____.

Election

Let's read a Bible passage which tells us more about the decrees of God:

Ephesians 1:11-12 In him we were also chosen, having been predestined according to the plan of him who works out everything in conformity with the purpose of his will, in order that we, who were the first to hope in Christ, might be for the praise of his glory.

This Scripture tells us that we were chosen by God and given salvation in Christ because God planned for this to happen so that we would glorify God.

 **Let's Think!**

Think back to the first lesson in this workbook. What is your main purpose?

_____

_____

According to Ephesians 1:11-12, what has God done so that we might be for the praise of his glory?

_____

_____

Those whom God has chosen for salvation in Christ are called his **elect**. These people have their hearts changed by God through the work of the Holy Spirit, and they are sealed as belonging to God. The next verse in Ephesians tells us how God marks us with his seal:

Ephesians 1:13 And you also were included in Christ when you heard the word of truth, the gospel of your salvation. Having

> believed, you were marked in him with a seal, the promised Holy Spirit.

Are you elect? _____

How do you know that you are elect? _____

_____

The apostle Peter wrote a letter to the elect (God's chosen people). He sent his letter specifically to believers in places called Pontus, Galatia, Cappadocia, Asia, and Bithynia. Here is how he began his letter:

> **I Peter 1:1-2**   Peter, an apostle of Jesus Christ, to God's elect, strangers in the world, scattered throughout Pontus, Galatia, Cappadocia, Asia and Bithynia, who have been chosen according to the foreknowledge of God the Father, through the sanctifying work of the Spirit, for obedience to Jesus Christ and sprinkling by his blood: Grace and peace be yours in abundance.

'Foreknowledge' means something is known before it happens. 'Sprinkling of his blood' refers to sins forgiven through the blood of Jesus Christ. Peter tells the elect that they were chosen by God through the work of the Holy Spirit which changed their hearts. God knew all of this and decided it before it happened.

According to this Bible passage, what should the elect do because they have been chosen by God?

_____

Did you become elect by doing good things? _____

Why are you elect? _____

_____

Who changes your heart so that you repent for your sins and obey God?

_____

God chose you and forgave your sins through the blood of Christ, so what should you do?

_____

_____

Lesson 3

Q. 7. What are the decrees of God?

A. The decrees of _____ are his _____

_____, according to the counsel of his _____,

whereby, for _____ own _____, he hath

fore-ordained _____ comes to pass.

Joseph and His Brothers

The book of Genesis tells a story about a young man named Joseph. The story begins when Joseph was seventeen years old. Joseph lived with his eleven brothers and their father Jacob (also called Israel) in the land of Canaan.

Genesis 37:3-36 Now Israel loved Joseph more than any of his other sons, because he had been born to him in his old age; and he made an ornate robe for him. When his brothers saw that their father loved him more than any of them, they hated him and could not speak a kind word to him.

Joseph had a dream, and when he told it to his brothers, they hated him all the more. He said to them, "Listen to this dream I had: We were binding sheaves of grain out in the field when suddenly my sheaf rose and stood upright, while your sheaves gathered around mine and bowed down to it."

His brothers said to him, "Do you intend to reign over us? Will you actually rule us?" And they hated him all the more because of his dream and what he had said.

Then he had another dream, and he told it to his brothers. "Listen," he said, "I had another dream, and this time the sun and moon and eleven stars were bowing down to me."

When he told his father as well as his brothers, his father rebuked him and said, "What is this dream you had? Will your mother and I and your brothers actually come and bow down to the ground before you?" His brothers were jealous of him, but his father kept the matter in mind.

Now his brothers had gone to graze their father's flocks near Shechem, and Israel said to Joseph, "As you know, your brothers are grazing the flocks near Shechem. Come, I am going to send you to them."

"Very well," he replied.

So he said to him, "Go and see if all is well with your brothers and with the flocks, and bring word back to me." Then he sent him off from the Valley of Hebron.

When Joseph arrived at Shechem, a man found him wandering around in the fields and asked him, "What are you looking for?"

He replied, "I'm looking for my brothers. Can you tell me where they are grazing their flocks?"

"They have moved on from here," the man answered. "I heard them say, 'Let's go to Dothan.'"

So Joseph went after his brothers and found them near Dothan. But they saw him in the distance, and before he reached them, they plotted to kill him.

"Here comes that dreamer!" they said to each other. "Come now, let's kill him and throw him into one of these cisterns and say that a ferocious animal devoured him. Then we'll see what comes of his dreams."

When Reuben heard this, he tried to rescue him from their hands. "Let's not take his life," he said. "Don't shed any blood. Throw him into this cistern here in the wilderness, but don't lay a hand on him." Reuben said this to rescue him from them and take him back to his father.

So when Joseph came to his brothers, they stripped him of his robe—the ornate robe he was wearing—and they took him and threw him into the cistern. The cistern was empty; there was no water in it.

As they sat down to eat their meal, they looked up and saw a caravan of Ishmaelites coming from Gilead. Their camels were loaded with spices, balm and myrrh, and they were on their way to take them down to Egypt.

Judah said to his brothers, "What will we gain if we kill our brother and cover up his blood? Come, let's sell him to the Ishmaelites and not lay our hands on him; after all, he is our brother, our own flesh and blood." His brothers agreed.

So when the Midianite merchants came by, his brothers pulled Joseph up out of the cistern and sold him for twenty shekels of silver to the Ishmaelites, who took him to Egypt.

When Reuben returned to the cistern and saw that Joseph was not there, he tore his clothes. He went back to his brothers and said, "The boy isn't there! Where can I turn now?"

Then they got Joseph's robe, slaughtered a goat and dipped the robe in the blood. They took the ornate robe back to their father and said, "We found this. Examine it to see whether it is your son's robe."

He recognized it and said, "It is my son's robe! Some ferocious animal has devoured him. Joseph has surely been torn to pieces."

Then Jacob tore his clothes, put on sackcloth and mourned for his son many days. All his sons and daughters came to comfort him, but he refused to be comforted. "No," he said, "I will continue to mourn until I join my son in the grave." So his father wept for him.

Meanwhile, the Midianites sold Joseph in Egypt to Potiphar, one of Pharaoh's officials, the captain of the guard.

The book of Genesis tells us many things that happened to Joseph after he was taken to Egypt. He was a slave in the house of Potiphar, but then he was falsely accused of a crime. Joseph was sent to prison for a long time, but God was with him through everything. Eventually, the Pharaoh released Joseph from prison and made him a rich and powerful man in Egypt.

One day, Joseph's brothers arrived in Egypt. They had traveled all the way from Canaan looking for food because of a terrible famine. When they realized that Joseph was now a powerful man in Egypt, they were afraid that he would take revenge on them for selling him as a slave. Joseph told them that he forgave them, and he gave food to them for their families. However, his brothers still worried that perhaps he was only waiting until their father died, and then he might kill them or sell them as slaves.

Finally, Jacob died. Joseph's brothers were terrified. The Bible tells us what happened:

Genesis 50:15-21 When Joseph's brothers saw that their father was dead, they said, "What if Joseph holds a grudge against us and pays us back for all the wrongs we did to him?" So they sent word to Joseph, saying, "Your father left these instructions before he died: 'This is what you are to say to Joseph: I ask you to forgive your brothers the sins and the wrongs they committed in treating you so badly.' Now please forgive the sins of the servants of the God of your father." When their message came to him, Joseph wept.

His brothers then came and threw themselves down before him. "We are your slaves," they said.

But Joseph said to them, "Don't be afraid. Am I in the place of God? You intended to harm me, but God intended it for good to accomplish what is now being done, the saving of many lives. So then, don't be afraid. I will provide for you and your children." And he reassured them and spoke kindly to them.

 ## Let's Think!

Did Joseph's brothers sin when they sold him as a slave?

_____

Did God plan for Joseph's brothers to sell Joseph as a slave?

_____

How do you know that God planned it?

_____

_____

Did God sin when he planned for Joseph's brothers to sell him as a slave? Why or why not?

_____

_____

Did Joseph always have a good life in Egypt? _____

What are some of the bad things that happened to Joseph in Egypt?

_____

_____

When Joseph was a slave or in prison, did this mean that God had forgotten him?

_____

How did Joseph explain to his brother's about God's decrees? What was God's reason for Joseph being sold as a slave in Egypt?

_____

_____

Even though bad things happen, we know that God is good. His purposes are always good. While Joseph was a slave, he did not know that God planned that someday he would save many people from famine. He had to simply trust God. Like Joseph, sometimes we cannot see the reason for God's plan immediately. The Bible tells us that we should trust God. His plan always works for good.

Romans 8:28   And we know that in all things God works for the good of those who love him, who have been called according to his purpose.

Question 8: How doth God execute his decrees?

Answer: God executeth his decrees in the works of creation and providence.

Lesson 1

Question 8: How doth God execute his decrees?

Answer: God executeth his decrees in the works of creation and providence.

Q. 8. How doth God execute his decrees?

A.

_____

_____

Creation and Providence

Why does the catechism say 'doth'? 'Doth' is an old word that means 'does.' This line could read: *How **does** God execute his decrees?*

Why does the catechism say 'execute'? In the way it is used in the catechism, 'execute' means 'work.' The term 'execute' can also mean 'kill,' so do not get confused on the meaning of that word! This question could read: *How does God work out his decrees?* or *How does God put his plans into action?*

 **Fill in the blanks.**

This section of the catechism tells us that God puts his plans into action through the works of:

_____ and _____

What is 'creation'? The term 'creation' refers to making things.

What is 'providence'? The term 'providence' refers to sustaining and providing.

God makes us, and he also sustains and provides for us.

God made the sun and moon. This is an example of (circle one):

creation   providence

God sends rain to make crops grow. This is an example of (circle one):

creation   providence

Lesson 2

Q. 8. How doth God execute his decrees?

A. God executeth his _____ in the works of

_____ and _____.

Do Not Worry

Let's look at some Bible verses about God's works of creation and providence.

Revelation 4:11 You are worthy, our Lord and God, to receive glory and honor and power, for you created all things, and by your will they were created and have their being.

What has God created? _____

In the gospel of Matthew, Jesus spoke about the providence of God. Let's read what he said:

Matthew 6:25-34 "Therefore I tell you, do not worry about your life, what you will eat or drink; or about your body, what you will wear. Is not life more than food, and the body more than clothes?

"Look at the birds of the air; they do not sow or reap or store away in barns, and yet your heavenly Father feeds them. Are you not much more valuable than they? Can any one of you by worrying add a single hour to your life?

"And why do you worry about clothes? See how the flowers of the field grow. They do not labor or spin. Yet I tell you that not even Solomon in all his splendor was dressed like one of these. If that is how God clothes the grass of the field, which is here today and tomorrow is thrown into the fire, will he not much more clothe you—you of little faith? So do not worry, saying, 'What shall we eat?' or 'What shall we drink?' or 'What shall we wear?' For the pagans run after all these things, and your heavenly Father knows that you need them. But seek first his kingdom and his righteousness, and all these things will be given to you as well. Therefore do not worry about tomorrow, for tomorrow will worry about itself. Each day has enough trouble of its own."

 Let's Think!

Who are the pagans? _____

What do the pagans worry about that we do not need to worry about?

_____

_____

Why do we not need to worry? _____

_____

Jesus gave two examples of ways in which God provides for his creatures. What are those examples?

_____

_____

Draw a picture of one way in which God provides for you:

Question 9: What is the work of creation?

Answer: The work of creation is God's making all things of nothing, by the word of his power, in the space of six days and all very good.

Lesson 1

Question 9: What is the work of creation?

Answer: The work of creation is God's making all things of nothing, by the word of his power, in the space of six days and all very good.

Q. 9. What is the work of creation?

A.

_____

_____

_____

_____

_____

The Work of Creation

God made all things. The book of Genesis tells us that he made the world and everything in it within six days and that he made it all from nothing. He spoke everything into existence. Everything that God made was good.

Fill in the blanks.

What did God use to make the world? _____

How did God create all things? _____

_____

God is good, and all things that God made were _____.

Lesson 2

Q. 9. What is the work of creation?

A. The work of _____ is God's making _____

things of _____, by the word of his _____,

in the space of _____ days and all very _____.

The Story of Creation

Genesis 1   In the beginning God created the heavens and the earth. Now the earth was formless and empty, darkness was over the surface of the deep, and the Spirit of God was hovering over the waters.

And God said, "Let there be light," and there was light. God saw that the light was good, and he separated the light from the darkness. God called the light "day," and the darkness he called "night." And there was evening, and there was morning—the first day.

And God said, "Let there be a vault between the waters to separate water from water." So God made the vault and separated the water under the vault from the water above it. And it was so. God called the vault "sky." And there was evening, and there was morning—the second day.

And God said, "Let the water under the sky be gathered to one place, and let dry ground appear." And it was so. God called the dry ground "land," and the gathered waters he called "seas." And God saw that it was good. Then God said, "Let the land produce vegetation: seed-bearing plants and trees on the land that bear fruit with seed in it, according to their various kinds." And it was so. The land produced vegetation: plants bearing seed according to their kinds and trees bearing fruit with seed in it according to their kinds. And God saw that it was good. And there was evening, and there was morning—the third day.

And God said, "Let there be lights in the vault of the sky to separate the day from the night, and let them serve as signs to mark sacred times, and days and years, and let them be lights in the vault of the sky to give light on the earth." And it was so. God made two great lights—the greater light to govern the day and the lesser light to govern the night. He also made the stars. God set them in the vault of the sky to give light on the earth, to govern the day and the night, and to separate light from darkness. And God saw that it was good. And there was evening, and there was morning—the fourth day.

And God said, "Let the water teem with living creatures, and let birds fly above the earth across the vault of the sky." So God created the great creatures of the sea and every living thing with which the water teems and that moves about in it, according to their kinds, and every winged bird according to its kind. And God saw that it was good. God blessed them and said, "Be fruitful and increase in number and fill the water in the seas, and let the birds increase on the earth." And there was evening, and there was morning—the fifth day.

And God said, "Let the land produce living creatures according to their kinds: the livestock, the creatures that move along the ground, and the wild animals, each according to its kind." And it was so. God made the wild animals according to their kinds, the livestock according to their kinds, and all the creatures that move along the ground according to their kinds. And God saw that it was good. Then God said, "Let us make mankind in our image, in our likeness, so that they may rule over the fish in the sea and the birds in the sky, over the livestock and all the wild animals, and over all the creatures that move along the ground."

So God created mankind in his own image, in the image of God he created them; male and female he created them.

God blessed them and said to them, "Be fruitful and increase in number; fill the earth and subdue it. Rule over the fish in the sea and the birds in the sky and over every living creature that moves on the ground." Then God said, "I give you every seed-bearing plant on the face of the whole earth and every tree that has fruit with seed in it. They will be yours for food. And to all the beasts of the earth and all the birds in the sky and all the creatures that move along the ground—everything that has the breath of life in it—I give every green plant for food." And it was so.

God saw all that he had made, and it was very good. And there was evening, and there was morning—the sixth day.

What a beautiful story! The language in Hebrew is almost like a lovely poem. It paints a vivid picture of God's work of creation. If you close your eyes and listen to the words, you can almost see it.

In the beginning, the eternal God was already there. The earth was empty and formless, but the Spirit of God hovered over the waters. And then ... (think of it!) .... God spoke: "Let there be light!"

And suddenly, there was light!

 **Fill in the blanks.**

List the things God made on each day of creation.

Day 1: _____

Day 2: _____

Day 3: _____

Day 4: _____

Day 5: _____

Day 6: _____

What did God do on the seventh day? _____

_____

What did God make in his own image? _____

Lesson 3

Q. 9. What is the work of creation?

A. The _____ of _____ is God's making all

things of _____, by the _____ of his

_____, in the space of _____ days and all

very _____.

What is Heresy?

   Heresy is wrong teaching about God.   Heresies are
dangerous because they can lead people into a wrong
understanding of God and of the world. A **heretic** is a person who
believes and teaches heresy (wrong ideas about God).

   We have talked about one heretic already.   Do you
remember Arius? (If not, look back at pages 58 – 61 in this
workbook.)

What was the heresy of Arius?

_____

_____

      Gnosticism is another heresy. People who believe Gnosticism are called **Gnostics**. Gnostics teach that matter (anything you can see and touch) is all evil and that only spirits are good. They believe that we achieve salvation by learning higher knowledge about the universe so that we can rise above our bodies and other material things to reach new spiritual levels.

      Let's consider how we know this idea is wrong.

 ## Let's Think!

Who made all the material things in the world (dry land, plants, animals, and so on)?

_____

What did God say about the things he created? _____

_____

Who formed the bodies of the first humans? _____

What did God say about humans after he formed them from the dust?

_____

Did God create bad things at all? _____

Did God ever say that spirits were better than the material things that he created?

_____

Everything that God created was _____.

Question 10: How did God create man?

Answer: God created man male and female, after his own image, in knowledge, righteousness, and holiness, with dominion over the creatures.

Lesson 1

Question 10: How did God create man?

Answer: God created man male and female, after his own image, in knowledge, righteousness, and holiness, with dominion over the creatures.

 **Q. 10. How did God create man?**

A.

_____

_____

_____

_____

In His Image

In this section of the catechism, you can clearly see that the word 'man' can refer to both men and women. It says that God created *man* both male and female.

Why does the catechism say that God created man 'after his own image'? God created men and women in some ways like himself. We are not God, of course, but we are made like him in certain ways. Notice that humans are the only thing God made like himself. Plants are not made in the image of God, and animals are not made in the image of God. But God created people to be like himself.

In what ways did God make man like himself? God created men and women to be like him in **knowledge** (what they know), **righteousness** (doing right things), **holiness** (purity), and with **dominion over the creatures** (ruling over the other things God made).

 Let's Think!

In what ways are we made like God? _____

_____

Do we look like God physically? Does God have arms, legs, eyes, and ears?

_____

Think of some things you can do that a plant or animal cannot do.

Can a dog plant seeds and tend a garden? _____

Can a tree read a book? _____

Does a fox ever think about whether it is right or wrong to steal a chicken from a farmer's yard?

_____

Name three more things you can do that animals and plants cannot do.

_____

_____

_____

Lesson 2

Q. 10. How did God create man?

A. God created _____ male and _____,

after his own _____, in knowledge, righteousness,

and _____, with dominion _____ the

_____.

Dominion Over the Creatures

The creation story in Genesis is beautiful. Another beautiful chapter about creation is found in Psalms:

Psalm 8

O LORD, our Lord,
how majestic is your name in all the earth!
You have set your glory above the heavens.

From the lips of children and infants
you have ordained praise
because of your enemies,
to silence the foe and the avenger.
When I consider your heavens,
the work of your fingers,
the moon and the stars,
which you have set in place,
what is man that you are mindful of him,
the son of man that you care for him?
You made him a little lower than the heavenly beings
and crowned him with glory and honor.
You made him ruler over the works of your hands;
you put everything under his feet:
all flocks and herds,
and the beasts of the field,
the birds of the air,
and the fish of the sea,
all that swim in the paths of the seas.
O LORD, our Lord,
how majestic is your name in all the earth!

 Let's Think!

This psalm was written by King David. What was David thinking about when he wrote the psalm?

_____

_____

What amazed David? _____

_____

David said that God had put what under the feet of mankind?

_____

_____

How does this reveal that man is made in God's image?

_____

_____

Lesson 3

Q. 10. How did God create man?

A. God created man _____ and _____,

after his _____ _____, in _____,

righteousness, and _____, with dominion over

the _____.

Mirrors of God's Glory

What does it mean to say that man is made in the image of God in knowledge, righteousness, and holiness, with dominion over the creatures?

John Calvin wrote about this concept in his book *Institutes of the Christian Religion*. Calvin was a theologian (a man who studies God). He lived during the Reformation, and he wrote many books to help people understand Scripture.

Calvin wrote about how we should understand ourselves as made in the image of God:

John Calvin, *Institutes of the Christian Religion in Modern English*, Book 1, Chapter 15:

Humans are created in the image of God. This is yet another proof of the existence of their immortal souls. Even our bodies differ from those of ordinary animals: "Other living things are bent downward toward the earth, but mankind has been given a face which is raised up to look toward the heavens and to gaze upon the stars." God's glory shines in the design of the human body, and there are whispers of eternity in everything around us, yet there is no doubt that the soul is the clearest reflection of God.

The astounding gift of human intellect reflects the glory of God. This is especially evident when we consider our restoration in Christ. When Adam fell, he was separated from God. God's image was not completely destroyed in him, but it was twisted and broken. In Christ, we are renewed. Jesus is called the Second Adam because He restores us to the full likeness of God.

Calvin explains how our special abilities (far above and beyond those of animals) are a reflection of God's glory.

The Westminster Shorter Catechism tells us what some of these abilities are:

1. **Knowledge.** God gave humans very complex minds with extraordinary abilities. Consider what you can do compared to what an animal can do. Some people claim that their dog is smart because it can roll over or bark when they give it commands. But a dog can never learn the catechism. You are much smarter than any animal. If you have a baby brother or sister, you know that even a little baby is smarter than a dog or cat or fish.

2. **Righteousness and holiness**. God gave humans the ability to learn and obey his commands. Animals and plants to not have the Bible. They do not think about whether things are right or wrong. Animals do things because they are hungry or playful or angry, but never because they are thinking about the Ten Commandments. Humans have a special ability to understand that we should obey God.

3. **Dominion over the creatures**. God made humans to rule over other creatures. We can grow crops, raise animals, and so on. Most children are born with a natural tendency to care for living things. Even little toddlers want to water flowers or feed a kitten. People keep dogs, cats, rabbits, fish, and other animals as pets in their homes. They mow their lawns and plant flowers. They do all these things because God gave humans dominion over the creatures.

Calvin pictures each person as a mirror. When you look into a mirror, you see an image of your face. We are like a mirror for the glory of God. God's glory shines in us, and we reflect his image.

 Let's Think!

Think back to the first lesson in this workbook.

What is your main purpose?

_____

_____

Why is this your main purpose?

I was created as a mirror of _____'s _____.

In which ways did God create humans as a reflection of his glory?

In _____, _____,

and _____, with _____

over the _____.

God created the first man and woman in perfect righteousness and holiness, with godly knowledge, and with dominion over the creatures. However, the first man and woman did not last long in this state of perfection.

Lesson 4

Q. 10. How did God create man?

A. God _____ man _____ and

_____, after his own _____, in

knowledge, _____, and holiness, with

_____ over the _____.

Shattered Mirrors

In the last lesson, we talked about how God created man to be a mirror of his glory. John Calvin says:

> Humans are created in the image of God. This is yet another proof of the existence of their immortal souls. Even our bodies differ from those of ordinary animals: "Other living things are bent downward toward the earth, but mankind has been given a

> face which is raised up to look toward the heavens and to gaze upon the stars." God's glory shines in the design of the human body, and there are whispers of eternity in everything around us, yet there is no doubt that the soul is the clearest reflection of God.

However, humans do not reflect God's glory in the way that they should. People do foolish things. They sin. They even sometimes fail at raising crops or caring for animals.

We will discuss this more in Workbook Two (*The Fall*), but you probably already know that Adam and Eve did not obey God, even though God gave them that ability in righteousness and holiness. Now humans are all **fallen**. They no longer perfectly reflect the image of God.

Let's review the rest of Calvin's comment:

> When Adam fell, he was separated from God. God's image was not completely destroyed in him, but it was twisted and broken. In Christ, we are renewed. Jesus is called the Second Adam because He restores us to the full likeness of God.

Calvin says that Adam became like a stranger far away from God. The image of God in Adam was not entirely lost, but it was twisted and broken.

Have you ever looked into a broken mirror? You can still see your reflection in the pieces, but it is smashed, jagged, and broken. This is similar to the way humans are now. We still have a lot of knowledge and some understanding of right and wrong. We still have some dominion over the creatures. But it is all imperfect. There is a lot of damage. Now some animals bite us and sting us. Sometime our crops fail. We often sin even when we know we should not. We can be foolish. Some people are so foolish that they do not even understand that God exists!

Calvin goes on to say that we are renewed in Christ. Jesus restores us and makes us new again so that we reflect God's image as we should.

 # Let's Think!

If you are renewed in the image of Christ, are you in the image of God? Why?

_____

What special title for Jesus does Calvin mention?

_____

Why do you think we refer to Jesus as the 'second Adam'?

_____

_____

This discussion of the broken image of God in mankind carries on in the next workbook *(The Fall)*. We will continue talking about Adam's sin and the devastating effect of this sin on mankind.

Westminster Shorter Catechism
Questions 1 - 10 Review

Q. 1. What is the chief end of man?
A. Man's chief end is to glorify God, and to enjoy him forever.

Q. 2. What rule hath God given to direct us how we may glorify and enjoy him?
A. The Word of God, which is contained in the Scriptures of the Old and New Testaments, is the only rule to direct us how we may glorify and enjoy him.

Q. 3. What do the Scriptures principally teach?
A. The Scriptures principally teach, what man is to believe concerning God, and what duty God requires of man.

Q. 4. What is God?
A. God is a Spirit, infinite, eternal, and unchangeable, in his being, wisdom, power, holiness, justice, goodness, and truth.

Q. 5. Are there more Gods than one?
A. There is but one only, the living and true God.

Q. 6. How many persons are there in the Godhead?
A. There are three persons in the Godhead: the Father, the Son, and the Holy Spirit; and these three are one God, the same in substance, equal in power and glory.

Q. 7. What are the decrees of God?

A. The decrees of God are his eternal purpose, according to the counsel of his will, whereby, for his own glory, he hath foreordained whatsoever comes to pass.

Q. 8. How doth God execute his decrees?

A. God executeth his decrees in the works of creation and providence.

Q. 9. What is the work of creation?

A. The work of creation is, God's making all things of nothing, by the word of his power, in the space of six days, and all very good.

Q. 10. How did God create man?

A. God created man male and female, after his own image, in knowledge, righteousness, and holiness, with dominion over the creatures.

To download the FREE solutions manual for his workbook, or to purchase the next workbook in this series, visit the Common Life Press website:

www.commonlifepress.org

Made in the USA
Coppell, TX
21 February 2022